Vietnam War

John Perritano

Created by Q2AMedia

www.q2amedia.com

Text, design & illustrations Copyright © Leopard Learning 2009

Editor Jessica Cohn
Publishing Director Chester Fisher
Client Service Manager Santosh Vasudevan
Project Manager Shekhar Kapur
Art Director Sumit Charles
Designer Shipi Sarkar
Art Editor Mariea Janet
Picture Researcher Shreya Sharma

10 9 8 7 6 5 4 3 2 1

ISBN: 81-907857-3-7

Printed in China

Picture Credits
t= top, b= bottom, c= centre, r= right, l= left

Cover Images: Front: The Image Bank: Getty Images
Back: Sgt. Robert W. Ingianni: DoDmedia

Half Title: Associated Press.

2 Bettmann: Corbis. 5 DoDmedia. 6 National Archives and Records Administration. 7 National Archives and Records Administration. 8-9 Larry Burrows: Time Life Pictures: Getty Images. 10 DoDmedia. 11 Associated Press. 12 Associated Press. 13 Army.mil. 15 Associated Press.

16 Associated Press. 17 CBS Photo Archive: Getty Images. 18-19 Archive Photos: Getty Images. 20 Associated Press. 21 Bettmann: Corbis. 22-23 DoDmedia. 23tr Associated Press. 24-25: Bettmann: Corbis. 26 Associated Press. 27 DoDmedia. 28 Bettmann: Corbis. 29 Associated Press. 31 U.S. Air Force Photo: Tech. Sgt. Jeromy K. Cross.

CONTENTS

POLISHED BLACK STONE

On a crisp fall day in 1982, thousands of military veterans met in Washington, D.C. The veterans gathered in remembrance of fellow soldiers who had died in the Vietnam War. They met to dedicate the new Vietnam Veterans Memorial. This was no ordinary memorial. Vietnam had not been an ordinary war.

THE GATHERING

Some of the veterans came dressed in **combat fatigues**. Others came in wheelchairs or on crutches. More than 58,000 names were etched into the monument's polished black stone. Each name memorialized someone who had died in the war. Many veterans touched the names of fallen comrades. Others wept. The memorial forced the nation to remember a war many wanted to forget. "It's like coming home," one vet said.

IN THE BEGINNING

Most U.S. troops sent to Vietnam served in the period from 1965 to 1971. They were fighting **communism**. Vietnam was a French colony until communist Vietnamese called the Viet Minh took over in 1954. International officials blocked a total communist takeover by dividing Vietnam into two. The communists were given North Vietnam. Non-communists were placed in charge of South Vietnam. Unwilling to accept the agreement, the Viet Minh decided that the North had to conquer the South.

FIGHTING BACK

Vietnam was a colony of France until World War II (1939–1945). During World War II, the Japanese occupied the region. After Japan was defeated, the French regained control. But the Vietnamese had grown tired of outside rulers. Vietnamese leader Ho Chi Minh and his communist followers, the Viet Minh, began a drive for independence.

War between North Vietnam and South Vietnam broke out in 1954. U.S. personnel began arriving to train South Vietnamese soldiers in 1961. The United States soon began military involvement in support of the South.

Visitors to the memorial leave photos and other tributes.

THE GULF OF TONKIN

U.S. officials feared what would happen if the communists gained control of South Vietnam. Officials thought the neighboring nations of Laos, Cambodia, Thailand, and Indonesia would also fall. The United States was concerned about South Vietnam's ability to defend itself against the North. The North Vietnamese army was stronger.

FIRST SHOTS

One of the early turning points came on August 2, 1964. On that day, a U.S. Navy destroyer was patrolling in the Gulf of Tonkin, off the coast of North Vietnam. North Vietnamese torpedo boats attacked the ship. Two days later, that same U.S. destroyer was attacked again. The North also attacked a second U.S. destroyer.

President Johnson (far left) visited the U.S. and South Vietnamese military.

BEGINNING IN THE GULF

The attacks on the ships in the Gulf of Tonkin led to increased U.S. involvement. The U.S. president at the time was Lyndon Johnson. The U.S. Congress gave President Johnson permission to send troops to Vietnam. From that day on, the American presence in Vietnam grew. When Johnson took office in 1963, there were only 16,000 U.S. troops stationed in Vietnam. By the end of 1965, more than a year after the Gulf of Tonkin incident, about 184,000 U.S. troops were "in country," or stationed in Vietnam.

Many more thousands of U.S. troops would follow. Many thousands would die. Millions of Vietnamese would die on both sides.

Soldiers were decorated for bravery in battle.

LYNDON JOHNSON ACTS

President Lyndon Johnson asked the U.S. Congress to give him the power to "take all necessary steps, including the use of armed force." Both the Senate and the House of Representatives passed the measure right away. Most members of Congress were supportive of the president. Senator Wayne Morse, of Oregon, on the other hand, called the move a "historic mistake."

ROLLING THUNDER

The war between the South and North heated up after the Gulf of Tonkin. President Johnson thought that a mighty show of U.S. force would cause the communists to back down. He believed that U.S. support would allow South Vietnam to remain a separate nation.

TAKING CHARGE

General Curtis E. LeMay was the U.S. Air Force's chief of staff. He favored an all-out aerial bombing campaign. LeMay declared that U.S. bombs could send North Vietnam "back to the Stone Age." Johnson supported the idea of a bombing campaign, but put limits on it.

FIRST COMBAT TROOPS

In March 1965, Operation Rolling Thunder began. The bombing campaign continued on and off for three years. U.S. bombers destroyed a weapons storage area just north of the border between North and South Vietnam. The first wave of U.S. combat troops came ashore on March 8, 1965.

ROLLING THUNDER

During Operation Rolling Thunder, U.S. warplanes destroyed bridges and other targets. The president and his advisers selected the targets to be bombed. The Americans dropped 1.3 million pounds of bombs during the operation. Yet, the campaign was a failure. The North Vietnamese rebuilt whatever the bombs destroyed.

U.S. officials started with an air war.

BATTLEFIELDS

Both sides geared up for ground war. By 1965, the North had established several bases in the South. These bases included a key spot on a peninsula near the South China Sea. In August 1965, U.S. Marines launched Operation Starlite, the first major military campaign of the war.

OPERATION STARLITE

Marines, supported by U.S. Navy ships, landed on the peninsula held by the communist **guerillas**, called the **Viet Cong**. The guerillas had stationed 15,000 soldiers at their base there. At first, the Viet Cong fought hard. Then they retreated in fear. After six days, the Marines killed 614 Viet Cong. The Viet Cong killed 45 Marines.

U.S. helicopters were called "horses."

THE AIR CAVALRY

In October, the U.S. air **cavalry** was sent to the highlands of the South. Helicopters played an important role in Vietnam. Outfitted with guns, these mechanical "horses" could carry troops into remote areas of combat. Helicopters could also hover at treetop level and fire at enemy troops. Helicopters **evacuated**, or removed, the wounded from the battlefield.

The Chinook helicopter was made for heavy lifting.

THE BATTLE OF IA DRANG VALLEY

In November 1965, the North decided to attack in central South Vietnam. The North set its sights on Ia Drang Province. Winning there would split the country, a strategic advantage. U.S. General William Westmoreland learned about the plan. He ordered the air cavalry into action. Colonel Harold G. Moore was the U.S. officer placed in charge. The North Vietnamese Army (NVA) attacked as Moore's troops were stepping off their helicopters on November 14. The fighting was hard and brutal.

The Americans called for help by radio. All available U.S. helicopters and airplanes came to the rescue. This airpower turned the tide of the battle. Moore's troops stopped the NVA from seizing central Vietnam.

HO CHI MINH TRAIL

The communists could not match the Americans in firepower. Yet, the North could match wits. To build their strength, the communists built up the Ho Chi Minh Trail. They used the trail to send supplies from North Vietnam to Viet Cong in the South.

The Ho Chi Minh Trail served as a supply route.

ON THE TRAIL

The Ho Chi Minh Trail was a system of roads, supply depots, and rest stops. The roadways cut through the **neutral** countries of Laos and Cambodia. The network of roads allowed the communists to attack nearly anywhere in the South. The trails eventually covered 12,500 miles (20,000 km). Women and children carried rice and weapons along the Ho Chi Minh Trail. Boys on bikes also moved supplies. The Americans and South Vietnamese tried to stop the flow of supplies. Most attempts failed.

THE DMZ

The five-mile-wide zone between North and South Vietnam was the **Demilitarized Zone (DMZ)**. The DMZ was supposed to be a border between two countries. Yet, once fighting broke out, the North repeatedly crossed the DMZ to supply its troops. To stop the North's border crossings, the U.S. launched Operation Die Marker. The U.S. plan was to build a 25-mile-long barrier along the DMZ.

The Ho Chi Minh Trail (marked in red) was really many trails.

The barrier was built with devices that sensed movement. The line had barbed wire, minefields, and watchtowers. The Americans never finished constructing the barrier, however. Some of the war's heaviest fighting took place near the DMZ.

UNCONVENTIONAL WAR

World War I had its "doughboys." World War II had its "G.I. Joes." In Vietnam, U.S. soldiers gave themselves the nickname "grunts." The name came from the sound the soldiers made while hauling heavy equipment on their backs.

NEW REALITIES

Many grunts thought the United States would win the war quickly. They were mistaken, because Vietnam was a different kind of war—a young man's war. The average age of the U.S. soldier was just 19. World Wars I and II were fought by somewhat older soldiers and with time-tested military **tactics**. In Vietnam there were no **front lines**. Instead, the enemy could be anywhere. Americans soon realized that old tactics would not work in the jungles of Vietnam.

The Americans realized that to win the war they would have to win the hearts and minds of the villagers. The U.S. military tried to rally the South Vietnamese to the American cause. But many villagers simply supported whichever side left them alone.

SPECIAL FORCES

The United States trained special groups of soldiers. They were taught to adapt to warfare in Southeast Asia. Among these groups were the Green Berets and Navy SEALs. These special soldiers gathered intelligence. They also directed gunfire and ran secret missions.

SEARCH AND DESTROY

Most of the fighting in Vietnam
took place between small groups
of soldiers. Generally 40 or fewer
fought. American G.I.s would go out
on "search and destroy" missions.
They would march in hopes of finding
the enemy. But sometimes the jungle
itself became an enemy. Soldiers often
suffered from "jungle rot," a severe
rash. The heat and humidity weakened
the American troops. It was also hard
for the Americans to tell who the
enemy was. The NVA wore uniforms,
but the Viet Cong looked like
civilians. Some Viet Cong were women
and children. The Viet Cong set **booby
traps** and ambushed U.S. soldiers.

*U.S. troops befriended
villagers when possible.*

DATELINE VIETNAM

Reporters and photographers from many newspapers, magazines, and radio stations covered the war. Historians often note, however, that Vietnam was the first televised war. Seeing images of war on television was new to people.

ON THE STORY

Covering Vietnam was difficult. Unlike today, journalists did not have computers, cell phones, or modern cameras. Instead, they filed their stories by telephone or by telegraph. Television crews carried big, bulky cameras. They filmed their reports and sent them to the networks.

Americans watched war reports on television.

UNDER FIRE

Reporters often traveled with soldiers on missions. Joe Galloway of United Press International (UPI) served 16 months in Vietnam. He was the only reporter with Colonel Moore during the battle of Ia Drang. When the fighting began, Galloway stayed on his stomach. He tried taking pictures without getting shot. "I was down as flat as I could get when I felt the toe of a combat boot in my ribs," Galloway said. One of the officers told me to stand. "'You can't take no pictures laying down there on the ground, Sonny . . .' I thought: 'He's right.'"

War reporters like Joe Galloway became household names.

Galloway stood up and took pictures. He survived the battle and filed stories about it.

WATCHING AND WONDERING

Television viewers who watched Vietnam war stories began to question the war. Never before had the horrors of battle reached so far into American homes. TV viewers saw dead soldiers and villagers. Audiences were especially shocked after watching a famous story by CBS's Morley Safer. In Safer's report, U.S. Marines torched a village with cigarette lighters. These and other images influenced public opinion in the United States.

ANTI-WAR MOVEMENT

In the early 1960s, public support for the war was strong. Later, support for the war decreased. Americans began questioning the war. By 1968, many Americans were convinced the time had come to bring the troops home.

IN PROTEST

Groups of Americans voiced their opposition to the war. The protesters included many college students. Other young Americans fled to Canada. They didn't want the government to **draft**, or force, them into the military.

DEMONSTRATIONS

Thousands of protesters began holding anti-war demonstrations. One huge march on Washington, D.C., drew 500,000 people. As public support fell, some members of Congress began questioning the war. Even some veterans coming home from Vietnam marched in protest.

Protesters often held "sit-ins." They would sit and not move.

JOINING FORCES

Civil-rights groups said the government needed to get out of Vietnam. They said we needed to help people at home. In 1967, Dr. Martin Luther King, Jr., said, "We have been repeatedly faced with the cruel irony of watching Negro and white boys on TV screens as they kill and die together for a nation that has been unable to seat them together in the same schools."

One of the most violent anti-war demonstrations occurred during the 1968 Democratic Convention in Chicago. Police beat and arrested hundreds of protesters. The violence was seen on TV. The protesters shouted, "The whole world is watching!"

THE TET OFFENSIVE

On January 31, 1968, millions of Americans watched the war news in horror. The U.S. embassy in Saigon was under attack. The attack was the beginning of a major communist effort. General William Westmoreland was saying that the United States was winning the war. Now, many Americans weren't so sure.

The Tet Offensive took place on the streets of Saigon and throughout South Vietnam.

BREAKING A CEASE-FIRE

The **offensive** took place during **Tet**, the new-year celebration in Vietnam. The holiday is the most important day on the Vietnamese calendar. Both sides agreed to stop fighting for three days. However, the communists used the cease-fire to launch a series of surprise attacks. The communists went after major cities and military bases throughout South Vietnam.

NEWS AT THE NEW YEAR

The short battle that raged inside the U.S. embassy in Saigon captured most of the world's attention. Viet Cong soldiers blew a hole in a wall and stormed inside. With TV cameras rolling, American defenders killed the attacking Viet Cong. But the firefight inside this symbol of U.S. power shocked the world.

The siege of Khe Sanh outlasted the rest of the Tet Offensive.

TET OFFENSIVE

The North thought they could inspire people in the South to rebel against their government. They wanted them to join the communist fight. The Viet Cong and NVA overran the ancient city of Hue. They surrounded a U.S. Marine base, targeting coastal cities that once had been safe from combat. The communists also went after Westmoreland's headquarters at the Saigon airport. The Tet Offensive lasted four weeks. It was a military failure for the North. Yet, the United States and the South did not win, either. The South Vietnamese did not rise up. The North lost more than 58,000 soldiers.

Four thousand U.S. troops died, along with 5,000 South Vietnamese. The images on TV angered many Americans, who believed the U.S. had lost the battle. After the Tet Offensive, American public support for the conflict dropped to a new low.

A Casualty of War

The fighting in Vietnam harmed Lyndon Johnson's presidency. President Johnson wanted to wage "A War on Poverty" in the United States. He wanted to run a program he called the "Great Society." Yet, Johnson also did not want to lose in Vietnam. The cost of trying to do everything strained the U.S. government and funds.

STALEMATE

By 1968, Vietnam had become a war of **attrition**. Each side tried to kill as many of the other side as possible. The president had promised Americans that the end of the war was in sight—a "light at the end of the tunnel." But Johnson and his advisers misunderstood that the North Vietnamese were willing to pay a huge price in human lives to continue the war. The communists were not afraid to die for their cause.

The number of U.S. troops in Vietnam reached a peak in 1968.

IN THE NEWS

Pressures mounted in the White House. The press was reporting that Vietnam was a **stalemate**. Members of the press said the U.S. could not win. Even some of Johnson's advisers told the president that sending more troops would do no good.

President Johnson was in the White House from 1963 to 1968.

THE NUMBERS

By the end of 1968, about a half million U.S. military personnel were in Vietnam. The U.S. **economy** was in trouble. Anti-war demonstrations and riots in American cities added to Johnson's problems. He was up for re-election in 1968. Several politicians in his own party were running against him.

In March 1968, Johnson announced that he would slow the bombing of North Vietnam. He asked that peace talks begin. Then the president stunned the nation, saying, "I shall not seek, and I will not accept, the nomination of my party for another term as your president."

HAMBURGER HILL

After the Tet Offensive, fighting decreased for a while. The Viet Cong and the NVA were low on supplies. In early 1969, the communists began stocking a major South Vietnamese base. The NVA wanted to use the South Vietnamese location, near the DMZ, for mission launches. The United States and South Vietnamese decided that it was a good time to destroy the Viet Cong fort.

APACHE SNOW

On May 10, 1969, the South and the United States launched Operation Apache Snow. On the second day of battle, American troops seized a hill near the fort. The North Vietnamese fought back hard. What happened next would be one of the most brutal battles of the war. U.S. troops called the battle a "meat grinder." History would call it "Hamburger Hill."

"WAS IT WORTH IT?"

A soldier wrote a letter home during the battle of Hamburger Hill: "I am writing this in a hurry. I see death coming up the hill."

DAYS OF DEATH

The battle raged for nine bloody days. When the fighting was over, 630 communists were dead. Fifty-six Americans had died. When troops cleared the hill of the dead, a U.S. soldier nailed a cardboard sign to a tree. It read, "HAMBURGER HILL." A second soldier added another sign: "Was it worth it?"

Although the Americans had won the battle, they soon abandoned the hill. A few days later, the communists returned and took the area back.

25

PRISONERS OF WAR

U.S. citizens were concerned about American prisoners of war. A treaty called the Geneva Convention had created certain rules for the treatment of prisoners during wartime. Countries were not allowed to torture, kill, or humiliate prisoners of war (POWs).

Most POWs were pilots of downed aircraft.

NO PROTECTION

According to international law, the POWs had to be treated humanely. Unfortunately, the North Vietnamese did not follow these rules. Entering World War II, the U.S. Congress had declared war. The U.S. government did *not* do this in Vietnam. The North Vietnamese government therefore claimed that American POWs did not fall under the protections of the Geneva Convention. The communists treated the POWs as criminals.

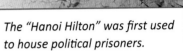

The "Hanoi Hilton" was first used to house political prisoners.

THE HANOI HILTON

One of the most infamous prisoner-of-war camps in North Vietnam was Hoa Lo. The camp was also known as the "Hanoi Hilton." Hanoi was the capital of North Vietnam. Prisoners at the Hanoi Hilton stayed in their cells for long periods. They were tortured.

In January 1973, North and South Vietnam finally signed a treaty. The North officially released its American POWs. One of the first prisoners set free was Air Force Colonel Robinson Risner. He had spent seven and a half years at the Hanoi Hilton. President Richard Nixon asked to speak to the colonel over the phone. When answering the call, Risner said, "This is Colonel Risner, sir, reporting for duty."

IN THE END

U.S. voters had elected Richard Nixon president in 1968. By then, most Americans did not support the war. Nixon was calling for "peace with honor." To put his plan in action, however, one of the first things Nixon did was *expand* the fighting.

NIXON'S ACTIONS

Nixon promised to withdraw U.S. forces from Vietnam. He called his plan **"Vietnamization."** U.S. troops gradually were to leave the region. The South Vietnamese would take over the fighting. Yet, Nixon ordered the bombing of neighboring Cambodia to stop the North Vietnamese from supplying its troops in the South. In April 1970, Nixon announced his order to invade Cambodia.

U.S. and South Vietnamese troops shared duties in Saigon.

PROTESTS ERUPT

Nixon's **escalation** of the war angered many. Protests erupted across the United States. In May 1970, a protest broke out at Kent State University in Ohio. National Guardsmen shot and killed several unarmed demonstrators. America seemed to be at war with itself.

TALK OF PEACE

Henry Kissinger was President Nixon's adviser. Nixon and Kissinger held secret meetings to try to get the North to the peace table. Nixon then ordered a massive bombing of North Vietnam. During Christmas 1972, bombs rained down on North Vietnam. At the end of December, the North Vietnamese said they would make an agreement.

In January 1973, North Vietnam, the United States, South Vietnam, and the Viet Cong signed an "Agreement on Ending the War and Restoring Peace in Vietnam." U.S. soldiers were to leave within 60 days. The North had to release all its POWs.

Both North and South Vietnam broke the treaty, however. They battled for two more years.

In April 1975, the last U.S. troops left Saigon. The image of the last American helicopter leaving the rooftop of the U.S. embassy was seen around the world. The Vietnam War was finally over.

GLOSSARY

attrition—the act of wearing down the opposing side by inflicting casualties

booby traps—hidden devices designed to harm an enemy

cavalry—U.S. troops in Vietnam who used helicopters (named after troops who used to ride horses)

combat fatigues—clothing soldiers wear to blend in with surroundings

communism—a social and economic philosophy characterized by a classless society and the absence of private property

Demilitarized Zone (DMZ)—enforced border, such as the one between North and South Vietnam created in 1954

draft—send into service in the U.S. military; also known as conscript

economy—system of producing and distributing wealth

escalation—expansion of a conflict

evacuated—cleared people out of a specific area

front lines—military positions in direct contact with an enemy; the positions most advanced

guerillas—those who conduct surprise attacks behind enemy lines

neutral—not taking sides in a conflict

offensive—military plan of attack

stalemate—deadlock; a situation in which further action is not possible

tactics—science of arranging military forces for a desired outcome

Tet—new-year festivities in Vietnam, based on lunar calendar

Viet Cong—communist guerillas in South Vietnam

Vietnamization—policy by U.S. President Richard Nixon to turn the fighting over to the South Vietnamese Army as U.S. troops left the battlefield

SOURCES

Books

Lyndon Johnson's War. Larry Berman. W.W. Norton & Company, 1989.

10,000 Days of Thunder, *A History of The Vietnam War.* Philip Caputo. Atheneum Books For Young Readers, 2005.

Vietnam, A History. Stanley Karnow. The Viking Press, 1983.

Vietnam War. DK Publishing, 2005.

Web

http://www.digitalhistory.uh.edu/modules/vietnam/index.cfm

http://www.nytimes.com/learning/general/specials/saigon/

http://www.pbs.org/wgbh/amex/vietnam/

INDEX